T0199138

FACE your GIANT

Janet Baird

ISBN: Softcover   978-1-9845-4651-7
         Hardcover   978-1-9845-4650-0
         EBook   978-1-9845-4652-4

Print information available on the last page

Rev. date: 08/14/2018

To order additional copies of this book, contact:
Xlibris
1-888-795-4274
www.Xlibris.com
Orders@Xlibris.com

Acknowledgement

I would like to thank God for being my inspiration in life and my husband, Kevin Baird, for always supporting me.

As Gabby saw the sign "Welcome to Ohio," she was overcome with emotion.

She was so excited to be moving just two doors down from her grandparents, but she was also sad knowing she wouldn't be seeing her best friend Leila any more. Moving from the sunny state of Florida to the cold state of Ohio was another big adjustment...

...But she *was* excited about the snow.

As Gabby and her family pulled into the drive of her grandparents' house, her grandmother sat waiting on the porch with a beaming smile on her face.

Gabby looked on, her eyes scanning the neighborhood. Across the street was a boy -who appeared to be about her age- playing basketball.

Basketball was one of Gabby's favorite sports- and she was pretty good. Gabby hoped that maybe he would ask her to play.

After dinner Gabby took her sketch pad and sat on the porch, searching for something to draw. She was then surprised when the young boy from across the street came out bouncing his basketball.

He looked her way and waved. Gabby walked over to him and introduced herself. "Hi! I'm Gabby... I just moved here from Florida".

The boy replied with a smile. "Hello... I'm Bralen. I have lived in Ohio all my life." As Gabby and Bralen began an anticipated game of basketball, she learned that Bralen was twelve just like she was. He told her all of the good things and the not-so-good things about her new school.

After their game, Bralen grinned and told Gabby she was "pretty good ... for a girl." Gabby was relieved to have found a new friend so soon in her new town and enjoyed the fun weekend with her grandparents.

Sunday evening came, though, and that meant tomorrow was her first day of school. Gabby began to feel *so* nervous!

Gabby looked around at the bus stop for Brelen but he wasn't there. As she stepped onto the bus a friendly girl named Chloe invited Gabby to sit next to her. As the bus began to pull away someone yelled "hold up' it was Bralen. Gabby was relieved- she had already made two new friends.

Three O'clock came and Gabby had made it through her first day. Luckily for her, Chloe was in all of her classes and quickly gave her the title of "New Best Friend".

However, not everybody was so welcoming to Gabby. Every day, a boy named Gavin began to take Gabby's sketch pad from her while she waited for the bus to go home.

Gabby would end up in tears, begging for Gavin to give her the sketchpad back. Chloe felt bad for Gabby, but she was too afraid to stand up to a bully like him.

As time went by, Gabby joined the softball team. She was relieved that her mom would pick her up-which meant she didn't have to worry about Gavin.

However, one day Gabby's mom was late... And there was Gavin, waiting to bully her by taking her sketch pad once again. She begged for him to give it back, but to no avail.

Suddenly, a familiar voice exclaimed, "Give it back!" There stood Bralen, boldly and unmoved by Gavin's charades. Gavin apologized and handed the sketchpad back to Gabby. Gabby was relieved, and also curious. *Why was Gavin so afraid of Bralen?* she wondered.

Gabby never mentioned the incident to her mother. Instead, she decided that she wanted to know Bralen's secret to being so brave.

Gabby found Bralen playing basketball, as usual. She approached him and asked, "Gavin is so much bigger than you... Why aren't you afraid of him, too?"

Bralen explained, "Gavin used to bully me, too. But one day in Sunday school we learned about the story of David and Goliath... Have you heard it?"

Bralen went on, and told Gabby the story he so well remembered:

"David was a sheepherder, and the youngest of eight brothers. But even with being the youngest, when he had heard of a giant that the *entire* army of Israel was afraid of, David told the king that he wanted to fight this terrifying giant. David found his courage because he knew that even though he was smaller, God would protect him.

When David stood before Goliath, the giant began to mock him. But David replied, you come to me with a sword, a spear, and a shield- but I come to you in the name of the Lord." Then, David put a stone inside of his sling, and it hit the giant in the head, causing him to fall to his death!"

Bralen continued to explain, "I thought about how everyone was afraid of Goliath and this gave him more power. I prayed every day for a week asking God to help me take down the giant in my way...

That Friday on the playground, Gavin grabbed a ball from my hands- but this time I took it back. Suddenly, my friends J.J. and Noah- and several others- began to stand beside me, and we outnumbered Gavin. Defeated, he finally walked away."

When Gabby went to bed, she thought about the story Bralen had told her. She began to ask God to help herself and her friends get rid of the giants in their lives.

The next morning, Gabby was up bright and early. She was going to Sunday school with Bralen- and she couldn't wait to share with him what God had showed her.

After Sunday school Gabby asked Bralen to bring some of his friends over to her house. Bralen did, and Chloe came over, too. Gabby explained what God wanted them to do to help stop the bulling.

Determined, Gabby explained: "We are going to start a group text. When you see someone being bullied, simply text the word GIANT with their location... We will all show up and surround the bully, and he will stop just like Gavin did for you, Bralen!" Everyone thought it was a great idea.

Gabby called her friend Leila back home. Leila loved the idea and started a group text at her own school. Gabby went on to start a blog for kids to share their experiences with bullies and realized that even though she was in a new place, God was using her to help others face their giants.

"Face your giant- you'll never be alone!" Oh, guess who joined our group? You guessed it. Gavin!

Printed in the United States
by Baker & Taylor Publisher Services